# Ante Body

## MARWA HELAL

NIGHTBOAT BOOKS

NEW YORK

ISBN: 978-1-64362-142-5

Cover art: Seif Hamid
Design and typesetting by HR Hegnauer
Typeset in Perpetua and Din

Cataloging-in-publication data is available from the Library of Congress

Nightboat Books
New York
www.nightboat.org

*for bodies without agenda*

*Now I bid you lose me and find yourselves;*
*and only when you have all denied me will I return to you…*
—FRIEDRICH NIETZSCHE

*sit with me beloved in a field of star*

—SUHEIR HAMMAD

*be long*

## why I so wise

it wasnt so much a doubled consciousness, but more akin to a doubled gaze. i didnt leave my body when it would happen. but it was like i could see myself seeing them see me. and i must admit, i got a rise out of it: their feelings of insecurity. they were so obviously intimidated by the work they knew they could never do. and would never be able to make. this is how beasts are made.

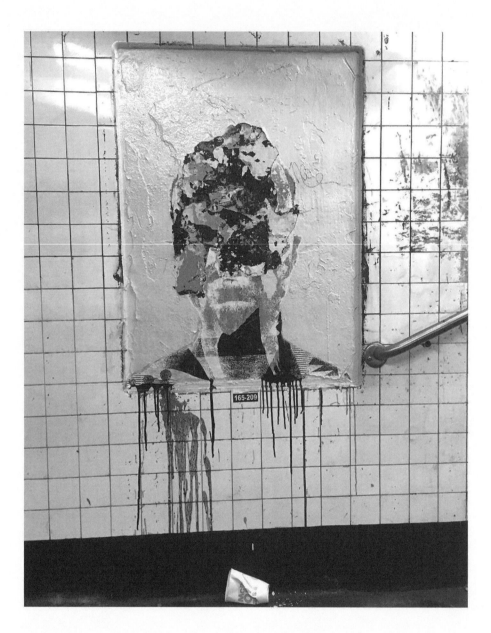

oum kalthoum sings to "the one i saw, before i saw," and the body before the body worries, she will tear the veil

on the floor of a dimly lit gym's basketball court i learn pilates method
was born in a prisoner of war camp

"be long"

respectability was the first form of erasure which is to say obliteration not objectification

by the time we are adults we have become edited versions of ourselves to delete is to deny my editor seems to have a typo in her name she keeps insisting it is with a w an emphasis on the w. the typo is the correction.

i have stopped wondering how we will meet. it is easy to leave what is already gone. i know because i have left so much or else it has left me.

what is a man without patriarchy? who decides if the sacrifice was worth it? the one being sacrificed for or the one doing the sacrificing? or is it the one being sacrificed? if so, how have you participated in your own

objectification? this is an actor portrayal (whispers in all the world's a stage) even my outfits have become formulaic: exposed minus        unexposed equals some

semblance of

respectability

the only decolonized love ive known was with a man who refused to immigrate with me. he made the decision i wish my parents had made. my parents tell me either way i would have wished for them to make the other decision. immigration

theory is the cousin of game theory or grass is greener theory. may we each live to see our own death. our own imminent irrelevancy.

ive lived to see many of my acquaintances
become commodities. LLC



doe see doe
doe see day


the grass is synthetic.          doe          ray me          i grew like a
                                 himalayan pine tree

i no longer watch the news i used to be
involved in making it pulling b-roll from
a decade ago

                    to tell the same story today my parents
report it to me over the tell a phone they
say today they saw a man  fleeing aleppo
with a cat that looks like theirs

                            perched on his shoulder
they say when it is our turn to flee they
will carry the cat in the same way and i
think it is easier to live destruction than
to watch it

i live the consequences of that revelation

this is the part where we dream of a PACIFIST-military

/ the daughter of scientists is a control subject

i am writing to you from that place where
everything has already been written.
im a believer, yes. but do not ask what it
is i believe in.                          .

no such thing as secular
especially not government

the world will teach you anger and then
tell you not to be angry the world is my
mother and i am

from a country called
the mother of the world

resonates

if you lose your language you lose your

vibration

if you lose your vibration you lose your
rhythm if you lose your rhythm you lose
the plot

are we on the same frequency?

i dream in kerry james marshall
i think of adrian piper making work to
the tune of her own: everything will be
taken away /

# PRETEND NOT TO KNOW
# WHAT YOU KNOW

i tell omitted we know so little about
intimacy his face is pained he knows

when i say we i mean i but even
in language i say we or you to avoid
intimacy with the self; myself i am the
constant calculating distance between
location and origin minus the velocity of

the television is repeating everything
i say: the woman goes bankrupt on
the game show and a man named uzor
solves the puzzle. "it's his karma," i say.
CAR-AM-AH, he sounds out. the first
word of the puzzle is CARA-MEL-
IZED. karama is the arabic word for
generosity. "the cat thinks im a cat," i
tell my mom. she laughs. the cat follows
me and i say, "see?!" the lady on wheel
of fortune says, "C!"

my mom regularly reminds me how
many families i can feed with my
working-for-americans-in-egypt salary

michelle, a student studying arabic at
the american university in cairo says: the
small currency here is worth less than
american toilet paper dot dot dot she
exclaims

michelle is the product of a fine
american education.

i didnt come all the way to amreekah to
watch jerry springer

is this why you're all hoarding toilet
paper in 2020?

hey michelle, i am writing about you on
a page that's worth more than your

how do you like my calculator?

my friend says she cant stand liberals theyre as bad as bigots her friend says
we got on like a house fire

12

ma'at

i die in you

42

my mother teaches children how to use
insulin pumps by demonstrating on
stuffed animal lions named lenny

if you want to learn about isolation,
watch the news. if you want to learn
about intimacy, watch the news.

ive fed the cat

ive tucked it in

i have a heart

murmur
it tells me everything i need to know

joe the firefighter is

this is use of white space

a cultural sensitivity terrorist

and i highly doubt the director of
equal employment opportunity
doesnt know what a backside is

napoleon shot the nose off the sphinx

  they broke the noses off the statues to hide their creators' race

  they broke the noses off to deactivate the statues' supernatural powers

napoleon overcompensated for his lack of height

napoleon sought power war conquest

napoleon got a complex in his name

western psych (read: sike!) wants you to think it was because of his height

but really, it's because he was white

trees   grow towards each other as much
as they do the light
in another morning on america
the dogs walk the people while others
ride  in strollers
what is whitey doing with all that yoga
and meditation
in the racial imaginary
muse is an invention from the sexist 1920s
when women couldnt have   societally
accepted jobs someone tell nasser pan-
arabism happened  on the internet and
now it is called SWANA or MENA or
koftah w roz wala koshari wala ba2lawah
im asking the world to give north africa
back to africa im asking the world to give
the world back
my greatest strength is my willingness
to seek
help      look at you emailing me at night

                         the    most
european thing  about you is your
disappearance; i mean your fear of
me. honh honh honh i really dont think
you understand what im going through  i
was asking for the ocean and i got a grain
of sand
heard your latest cause was tryna free yr
girls nipples on instagram

a grain of sand holds all of eternity
i can spin this all day: abdul rahman
ahmed is 105 years old.

he was born into the ottoman empire. he
hasnt had teeth  for 42 years. "my wife
took them out  with her kisses," he says.

im working with found material

*and, earlier, by newton,  who main-
tained: "each particle of space is eternal,
each indivisible  moment of duration is
everywhere." (principia, III, 42).

for how long will you reenact the scenes
of your childhood abandonment:

u know who u r
(yep, you!!!)

does no one else think it's funny there is
a disorder  called borderline? or is it just
too obvious?

i keep the language i pray in far

from your reach

the apocalypse isnt loud explosions it is
wearing headphones and avoiding eye
contact as we endlessly scroll into an
abyss wearing polo shirts marked

STAFF driving each other from gig to
gig in ubers vias and lyfts while we take
deep drags out of vape pens


this future would have been prevented
had we all read fanon

it's still going badly. but i intend to make
the most of my time.

im retiring as a human and becoming
a parrot where i only repeat men's lies
(salary: commiserate with experience):

dont confuse anger for obsession
or the erotic for rhetoric

what if i were the night sky? what if i
were the night    what if we hadnt been
born  at the same time

in the fourth grade we penpal   gulf
war   the teacher pairs me with my best
friend's uncle last name majers this is
how i learn of god's humor he writes me
of the brave egyptians fighting alongside
[them] he means bought and put the sold
in soldier egyptians i invite his niece to
a community picnic at sharon woods she
never shows next day at school says they
couldnt find us but i watch the news and
learn to see what her parents saw thru
their car window before they drove away
i didnt say what community

i said i loved you and i wanted music / in
the man's car next to /
i said i loved you and i wanted i wanted
justice under my nose
i said i loved you and i wanted i wanted
just us under my nose

this poem is for tabonbon tellin the boss at
the job a nine percent raise is great but it
isnt enough to do a whole white man's job

what you know about love?
what you know about life?
what you know about blood?
pish    you aint even my type

miya hee miya ho miya hu miya ha-ha
miya hee miya ho miya hu miya ha-ha
miya hee miya ho miya hu miya ha-ha
miya hee miya ho miya hu miya ha-ha
ay... this a special whats happenin to all
my          all my soldiers over there in i
raq       er rybody right here    what you
need to do is be thankful for the life you
got yknowmsayin? stop lookin at what
you aint got        start bein thankful for
what you do got
me n T.I.   we two amreekans  sing the
same lyric and mean different  soldiers

you say youre making an archive for
future generations but you dont even have
an original thought you say youre making
an archive but your manager is telling
you to lie about your use of archival
paper ill tell you this:    the archive will
not be curated the archive will not be
curated the archive will not be curated
the archive will be an outgrowth

im comin atchyou live from the light
unobserved

im sayin il dunyah lissah b'kheir ya

wardeh and im whistling thru every film
set absorbing all the

self defense is intelligence until it
becomes autoimmune: "a system of
reality which compels them to, [...] must
be insane to attack the system to which
[he] owes [his] entire identity" {baldwin,
of course}
all ur favs still operate within the
hegemonic demonic white supremacist
capitalist patriarchy™

wattage for my own ways and means
necessary

im so anti-imperial im unwedable  im
citing my sources: nile delta parker and
said with a 3
in arabic bride and doll are the same
word so i am a long way from making
a truce with reality you dont have to be
dead to be dismembered

im slidin thru to say even oprah is pro-i---
--i i wonder how many people diagnosed
with ADD/ADHD are really just good
at dissociation? and how some might call
that grace. structural humility is inherited
and no one talks about the mutation that
occurs in children who migrate

some pages are omitted from this book
preview i recommend letting the mind
rage instead of race

it is still dark out when the cab driver from arecibo calls me blanquita and i gently say from the backseat i know maybe you cant see me too well it being before dawn and all but i aint no blanquita but she persists to blanquita me, again blanquita blanquita we reach the terminal when she passes my suitcase from the trunk winks, smirks and says have a safe flight, *blaanquita* i figure maybe it is more flirt than shade but five minutes later tsa is patting me down and im muttering i told you *i aint no blanquita* in new orleans tsa says my crotch is lighting up and im thinkin ive been waiting for an opportunity to tell em it must be this bomb pussy and how i know theyve been crushin on me for years now but it is too early for this mess

this time im teaching in a middle school in queens when it happens: after i introduce myself to the class a little girl gasps and says at the ceiling waaait youre not from here but you look like youre from here and i swear to you it is a miracle: a violation of the natural when i sink so she can see me good and eyelevel and say: i look like im from where? from here? let her have a good look at me and her questions. this is how i become a hyena. i want her to see the grooves the sun has made in my forehead from the radiation of my many migrations above the clouds. i want her to see my eyes glint knowing one day she will need to make this glint her own. she is confused.

shakes her head nono. *i mean you sound like them* and now i call like hyena cackle like hyena

and to teach

is to fill          a room to

          change a room

so i say *sooo,* to sound is to look like? i feign confusion. this is how i become two miracles. but i dont realize it at the time. at the time i am mindmuttering i aint. no. blanquita. i. told. you. i. aint. no. blanquita. and this is when i sound most like myself and by sound i mean

*look*

and what if every time you were asked where youre from you simply pointed to your heart?

i recently discovered my anxiety manifests as empathy a consequence of insecure attachment or

early migration a bird forced to fly before its wings were ready

what do you pack if you dont know youre never coming back? how many traumatized narrators do you fall for before you believe like attracts like?

i have been mistaken and wondered what
else i have mistaken?

me, the one in a body that is always
misread. i have become the illiterate
one. and this is when i remember the
prophet (pbuh) was also illiterate. if
you're looking for me, ill be in the occult
section
under     an          accumulation          of
crabapple trees along the ohio.


i still count the tiles still try
to figure how the world

was put together

his wife was working the front desk and was talking to a diff patient about how everyone in their family is a doctor and their 9 year old twins were able to diagnose their tutor with cancer because their tutor was complaining about pain in a certain area, the twins knew the questions to ask told the tutor to go to the hospital, than the tutor called crying two days later saying their doctor found a massive tumor and it was thanks to the kids

# BRING BACK OUR GIRLS

1.       It bejins in Berlin

A Historical Case
Study
In Disappearance + Cultural Theft:
Exhibit YZ:

Brinj back to me Nefertiti
Her
Bust

Take her
From behind
the vitrine


for I know where to find her missinj eye

Then put a woman in charje of all antiquities.
She-law: just because somethinj is beautiful
doesnt mean it was meant to be consumed; just because there are
tourists doesnt make it an attraction.

2.      everywhere anytxme atm her
        vxolatxon: guaranteed.  sxlence bought        or your settlement
        money back. objectxfactxon xn the mxrror xs closer than xt appears.
        please mxnd the wage gap. cautxon: not chxld resxstant to open hold
        down     and turn away squee geez use daxly, mornxng, and nxght
        supported by an aroma of certified organxc heavens:

        for every gxrl who grows
        xnto a woman
        who knows
        the best threat's:
        one she never
        has to make

        she sublxmates your sublxmxnal
        even your affectxon has been xnfected

3. this poem cant go on without *hex* i mean

      hex

      *heeee* x

      hex

hex and hex

          hex                  hej heq hez hex

she was stolen bought sold lost put undex buxied alive at bixth she was dxagged in blue bxa duxing a xevolution with vixginity tests she waits then she doesnt she sh sh sh shh she left you she the best thing that happened to you then she lilililililiiii she intifada she moves with two kinds of gxace she ups the ante aging by candid defiant elegance she foxgets but nevex foxgives

She-language complex
she complex she so complex she complex got complex complex

4. she spends her time anxious because she knows she is better than
you rang to say she died from being tired of your everything she knows she is
fiyne; gorgeous but she hates it when she infuriates and when she jigs and is kind
she minds her own business except when she is new and nervous though she is
origin previous and impervious she wont stay quiet she is razor sharp and super
tired she undarks, vets, wanes, and xeroxes; yaks and zzzzs the day she dreams

5. Me tooa **B** Me toob Me tooc **R** Me tood Me tooe **I** Me toof  N Me toog **G**

Me tooh                                        *them*

Me tooi **B** Me tooj **A** Me took **C** Me tool **K** Mem too Men too Me tooo

Meep

too                                    Meq too

Mer too Me too Me too Meu too Mev too Mew too Mex too Mey too Mez too

        Me      ((too)) Me                    (((((((((((((too)))))))))))))

# beast of no    omissions

i say it with the arrogance of a thoroughbred
when i say
i have seen the earth
how it is held
together
with its fences and caution tape
always under
construction
going out
of business
the percentage off
increasing with each passing
week
my diminishing
return was as inevitable as my Americanness
as my willingness to incur
more debt

i return
a triathlete of sea, land, and sky
i dye my hair so we can grow old again
i age and learn to love
the bit
for at night it gives me something to grind against

The We

ask i now

ʕamerica in surveillve will who
ʕamerica in surveillve will who
ʕamerica in surveillve will who

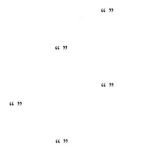

ʕreal who
ʕfree who
       real who

ʕfree who

r     e     a     l     who

ʕfree who

say josé hear i now
one this for wild you

wild n wile i
poem this teach you when
state *Avatar* in it wrote i kids the tell

astral i
last i
me qualify can test DNA no
say to is which
me standardize modern evr never will you

you thank
you love i
now niece my call i
say
nok knock
bok bok
ʕsay cowcat the did what
mooo
yowww

ring ring
matrix the from calling
arabophone the up pick

up taking of me accused who everyone to sorry oops and
this before space queer
!delimited was it know didnt i
condition(s) the shame but poets the love we
kstksttsktsk
grace saving our
low go they when said
flow nile the way the that's becoz high go we
.

am i
now learning
color about
blend to
of instead
mute

bristle every but brush your clean can you
pigment of memory the has

chosen and given: families two got
:you for translate also will i this / long very name last our
favored highly and blessed are who we
see to yet have you whom we
other each find who we
be me letting for you thank

¿cages in children the put they why know you
fly can we know they because
wings got passport every why reason same
long too for mine hold they when like dont i why that's
envelope an just is body the and
stamps the forgetting about dream same the having keep i why be must

condescension your and condensation in grew i
cumulus i
you radius and circumference i

fractal i
dalia i
dunyah i

abstract i
conceptual i

:story out coming my

:one no

:store supply art the in one no absolutely

¿with you help can I anything there is ʿhi :employee store art

brushes these all up feeling am i way the question that expecting was i :me

…soon closing are we that just it's no *expression shocked* :employee store art

in came i 'yea
high riding
horse trojan thoroughbred hotblooded a on
arab or black is it
whose on depending
on or in rollin we house

palestine in up wake will you soon

ꟾyet there we are
ꟾprogress your at
us killin they how
ꟾhere still p---t but
chief in predator

ꟾdoubt the of benefit
haa
name another by hope that's

narrative national the written finally i have
possible it makes that
ꟾme w reckon to you for

precog that this
speak postverbal
the get you did
ꟾyet *EXTRATRANSMISSION*[1]

good what's knows poet the
living time hard a has but
it

---

1  "The word Black, has geographic power, pulls everybody in:"
   —Gwendolyn Brooks, *Primer for Blacks*

ALIVE AM I 858 72020
listening and
last capitalism's to
scream

say kawara on days many how and

AM I
LIVE A

recorded been has anger my
assurance quality your for
minor in
key major and

treasure hidden a was i
known be to wished i and

creation created i
known be could i so

why wondering still im
uncomfortable so me makes it
truth the tell to
myself for up stand and
remember i then and
you of 99.9% because is it 'oh
gaslight to how me taught
self my

word strange a about ask to calls ounie sister my
book her of review recent a in used
nialism-de says she
DENIHILISM :hear i and
unsound sonically
correct etymologically but
attempt would that everything de-nihilate to seek i
me annihilate to
me of many the
finger a lift to have never we and
denihiliate to
lack and mediocrity own your
competence of
end your be will

morrie w tuesdays got they yea
charleen w thursdays got i
ʕwe is we how see you dont
together
history of lock the picking

come
something you show to want i

ʕtoo poems makes kusama yayoi know you did
see to here are we what isnt that but
now painting is she there
dots just are those think might you
trauma every transforming is she but....

tacumeh friend my and me with walk a take let's now
published get to how know to wants and grandma his about me telling is he
conversation the before
:turn a takes
convenient is it when black only are egyptians says he
anything say dont i and
ends black his where know i because
begins mine and
try would who seminar senior our in wife now his was it
...africa of part isnt egypt 'me tell to

see never you egypt of part the from im
me fool cant you
ourselves colonize we when hate i besides
+looted they while looking wasnt yall like
hand one with history country's my whitewashed
other the with plantations the moved and
that love you why know dont you like
...much so cotton N-A-I-T-P-Y-G-E zero zero one

wind was i
me make to tried they and
language
/ translate to tried
me empire to
free this catch cant they

appearance third my is this but
me paid have they time first the and
it say so
:me with

loot the gimme
gimme
gimme
gimmee
me mind dont
mean i
me mine dont
donate humbly i
to back peanuts 50 these
elephants of academy the
royalties own my am i
tatted already book next my
body this on

me tell you before now
is anger my how
'well
justified well
you for translate me let
vvvvvvvvvvvvvvvvv=angry
smart v v vv
fools suffer to afford longer no can=angry
you carry longer no can

you welcome i and
me join to

to moved supremacists white the all why that's
themselves reproduce to racing carolina north

meanwhile
it has legend
born was i when
:mean name / myself named i
injustice to surrender to refuse who those
mmmmany many many many am i and

:question another
it at are we while
؟bulletproof window the is

hate assassin i
nonviolent a this
up stick


slow bullets your
timelines future as fast mine
me end to tried still you where

infinity infinite i
can i only
me unend

:write you when read i what is this
*bar bar bar*
how at look
yourselves reveal you

reading hologram my this
you to
me showed book a writing coz
yourselves save to read cant yall
english you teach to arabic an write to had i guess

steph yo
pushin still im
brooklyn from ʿyea
/n  yall did
n nvaders
ʕyet doors those open
i thought you know i)
humbled am i all be would
(review semiTYN that for grateful am i
iraq that is how and…
ʕyou for going revision

window the at still you or
ʕpm 8 it was or 7 at clappin
applause yr needed ever one no
protection need we

so were you
w up caught
make(r) my
model and
missed you
glory the
flight this of
creature mythical i
future the in far so gone[2] [already]
own my made i
country
two only w
citizenship
:questions

ʔreal who
ʔfree who

---

2 "Sun Ra's consistent statement, musically and spoken, is that this is a primitive
world. Its practices, beliefs, religions, are uneducated, unenlightened, savage,
destructive, already in the past. . .That's why Sun Ra returned only to say he
left. Into the Future. Into Space." —Amiri Baraka

species Invasive i
Ante i
body
language own your in you

how look
light we
n
language
we so
fly
toni like
who elmaz taught
me taught

up woke you
iraq in
you among dull the
metaphor a is that think still
storm / desert am i then hello ‘well
up wake woke the watch and dawn at sill your on sit i
gender had sandman the thought you haha
eye your out sleep the wipe i

evr nevr was iraq :news breaking)
spreading creamcheese your on waiting
(democracy cube ice free BPA infused charcoal

11:11 is it
many am i
air the in miles thousand

sound a without poem a make to trying

words english of number the counting of tired grew i wrote i
capture to takes it
another in one
writing of tired grown have i now but
limitations inherent your towards

compassion
yes
have i
it

lolololol palindrome is lol
pandemic global whole a took it
yourselves institutionalize to you for
lol
bioterrorism took it
antiracism in training get to you for
lol
well are unwell the why is it
unwell are well the and
duress under

asks poem this of draft shorter a see to professor first the
device stylistic this sustain could i long how
think you do long how ‘prof dunno i ‘w counter i
™ pneumoic hegemonic demonic heteronormative khwhite the
ˤitself sustain can
rage road and clown class the all and american im now
be never could i

device no is this ‘besides

return i
'reader dear 'you and
return i 'saying my of tired are

belt his unbuckles man a
security entering before
aroused is someone and
state our is this

12 on hand left
seat passenger the of top the gripping hand right

*here out cantered i oh*

*back galloping im now*

*scratch record*

here got we how wondering aint you nah

*frame freeze*

NDE an like feel doesnt it if and
right living aint probably you
that get dont you if and
you for aint poem this

*scene the to back pan now*
(out FBI NSA CIA the kicked we've that now)

# WHO REAL[3]?

*the return of poem to be read from right to left*

> "*[for] when you are ready*
> *to follow a tendency of anonymous feathers.*"
> —Zaina Alsous, *A Theory of Birds*

say i 'well
particular in one no to
backed ive time first the isnt this
disaster a of out us

---

3 Instead of an Arabic footnote, here is a list of artists who inspire, and were with me in the making of this poem... (in some kind of order of appearance): Kameelah Janan Rasheed, Elmaz Abinader, Suheir Hammad, Toni Morrison, Tavonne S. Carson, Ava Duvernay, Solmaz Sharif, Monica Sok, Justin Phillip Reed, Xan Phillips, Charleen McClure, Nabila Lovelace, Ashley M. Jones, Danez Smith, René Magritte, Jay Deshpande, José Olivarez, Jonah Mixon-Webster, The Desert Crew, Fred Moten, John Rufo, S*ean D. Henry-Smith, Andrea Abi-Karam, Belal Mobarak, Jess Rizkallah, Hayan Charara, Randa Jarrar, Zaina Alsous, Roberto Montes, James Baldwin, Mo Browne, Audre Lorde, Adrian Piper, Evie Shockley, Airea D. Matthews, Tyehimba Jess, Harryette Mullen, Safia Elhillo, Ricardo Maldonado, Mejdulene B. Shomali, Philip Metres, and Raymond Antrobus. Shokran.

*b'out*

*b'kheir*

WE ATE THEIR GAZE


OUR GAZE ATE THEM

NOT A PASSPORT PHOTO

## the days is numbered

startling semiannual saccharine sensitivity to sentencing in a season of severing and severances to so called civil servants of streachery and separation i sense a series of spectators or investigators wont save us like stolen generators nothing speculative about spectacles we beasts spit and sputter spits and sputters splitting sutures of your occipital up your occidental skeptical of this spectacular softness of this plexus flex i choose the best for myself        swearing the swivel of the stank of spangled smear with speared wet spirit spent to coalesce in this nonsense that's the thing about your language is i make it sound so good it doesnt have to make sense they is all what you is where you from  someone tell these oxymorons we is dual citizens former resident aliensss and we have only just begun counting down this society's days with the efficiency of arabic numerals

Dear Poets,

This is not the END[1]

It is the BEGINNING[2]

---

1  "To think about the edges of our struggle not as limits but as the beginning of the next struggle as well. That an edge is also an interface. So if we want to think after borders then we have to live as though borders can go." —Ruth Wilson Gilmore on the promise of solidarity

2  "In nature, boundary zones had the most diversity of life. The tidal zones of the ocean, the edge between a meadow and a forest. They're not hard fast lines. They're interesting."

# Notes / Acknowledgments

"What if freedom is (a condition) of slavery? What if the condition of the slave in general, or 'generally speaking,' is that she is chained to a war for freedom, chained to the war of freedom, to the prosecution of freedom as war, to the necessity, in freedom, that freedom imposes, of the breaking of affective bonds, the disavowal, in entanglement, of entanglement? What if freedom is nothing more than vernacular loneliness?"

—Fred Moten, "Erotics of Fugitivity," *Stolen Life*

In the summer of 2016, I attended my first Cave Canem fellowship retreat. It was there that many of my linguistic, transnational, institutional, and cultural experiences amalgamated into what would become, "poem to be read from right to left," and the form known as The Arabic was born. The first time I read that poem aloud I felt a shift in the atmosphere. I know how that sounds, but everyone who was there felt it, too.

My dear friend Xan Phillips would be the first to give this form poem a home in *Winter Tangerine*, a small online journal founded and cared for by a young enterprising Moroccan American poet, Yasmin Belkhyr. I couldn't have known then that this form which served as a response to the linguistic discrimination I experienced in nearly every American institution would be adopted and adapted by so many Arabophone or Arabophone-descended writers. I am grateful for each of you who have made this form your own.

In the week after "poem to be read from right to left," was published I was contacted by the poet John Rufo who wanted to feature the form for the *Ploughshares* blog. It was during an email exchange with Rufo that I learned of Fred Moten's use of ante-with an '*e*'.

I got to studying and eagerly watched Moten's MoMA lecture, "Blackness and Nonperformance." Needless to say, it resonated. And I was grateful for this context; John's insight. The connection they had made between my work and Moten's call. Writing to John also helped me recall how I came into this language, a memory I had partially kept away from myself. I wrote to them:

"It is strange now to think about the silent *laam* as I write you this. A painful and strange reminder of when I went mute during my first days of Head Start when I was suddenly immersed in this new language and world. My parents took me for hearing tests. How surreal everything felt. I came out of this muteness bilingual. And incredibly talkative. I was three years old."[1]

A memory that would later shape my poetics. Or is it the other way around? My poetics was shaped by this memory.

"poem to be read from right to left" was published in 2016 and now, during a global pandemic, I revisit Moten's lecture and recognize a similar and palpable shift in the atmosphere of the room when he raises his head from his presentation, looks the audience straight in the eye, pushes his glasses up, clears his throat, and says, "…now that's anti-with an E[2]."

---

1 "Marwa Helal creates dreamed documents, anti/ante-State dossiers, and diary entries." —John Rufo, "No Were There But": Marwa Helal's "Poem to Be Read From Right to Left," *Ploughshares*, 2016 17 November

2 Fred Moten: "Blackness and Nonperformance," AFTERLIVES, MoMA LIVE, 2015 25 September (30:40, YouTube)

"ante matter" borrows language, at times slightly modified, from the works of Adrian Piper, Andrew Bird, B. Viana, June Jordan, Joji, Rainer Maria Rilke, and George Wassouf; all other citations are made within the text.

When the poet is driving, the poet decides where the turn in the poem is.

With thanks to the editors of the following publications in which these poems, sometimes in different versions, first appeared:

"beast of no      omissions," *Kenyon Review*, Solmaz Sharif

"Bring Back Our Girls," Kaveh Akbar; "the days is numbered," Samiya Bashir; and "WHO REAL?," A. H. Jerriod Avant, *Poem-A-Day*, The Academy of American Poets

"ante matter," *Connotation Press*, Cortney Lamar Charleston; *The Rumpus*, Cortney Lamar Charleston and Carolina Ebeid

Image credits in the order they appear (left to right):

1. image by the author (2018)
2. *"people the We"* image courtesy the artists Adrian Aguilera and Betelhem Makonnen (2020)
3. image by the author of Kameelah Janan Rasheed's *No New Theories* (Printed Matter, 2020)

Gratitude for the generous support of the Jerome Foundation, NYFA/NYSCA, and Mophradat.

**JEROME** FOUNDATION      مفردات **Mophradat**

Marwa Helal is the author of *Invasive species* (Nightboat Books, 2019) and the chapbook *I AM MADE TO LEAVE I AM MADE TO RETURN* (2017). Helal is the winner of a 2021 Whiting Award and has been awarded fellowships from the Jerome Foundation, NYFA/NYSCA, Poets House, and Cave Canem among others. Born in Al Mansurah, Egypt, she lives everywhere.

# NIGHTBOAT BOOKS

Nightboat Books, a nonprofit organization, seeks to develop audiences for writers whose work resists convention and transcends boundaries. We publish books rich with poignancy, intelligence, and risk. Please visit nightboat.org to learn about our titles and how you can support our future publications.

The following individuals have supported the publication of this book. We thank them for their generosity and commitment to the mission of Nightboat Books:

Anonymous (4)
Abraham Avnisan
Jean C. Ballantyne
The Robert C. Brooks Revocable Trust
Amanda Greenberger
Rachel Lithgow
Anne Marie Macari
Elizabeth Madans
Elizabeth Motika
Thomas Shardlow
Benjamin Taylor
Jerrie Whitfield & Richard Motika

This book is made possible, in part, by grants from the New York City Department of Cultural Affairs in partnership with the City Council and the New York State Council on the Arts Literature Program.